Gallery Books
Editor Peter Fallon

A FOOL'S ERRAND

Dermot Healy

A FOOL'S ERRAND

Dermot Healy (signature)

Gallery Books

A Fool's Errand
is first published
simultaneously in paperback
and in a clothbound edition
on 16 September 2010.

The Gallery Press
Loughcrew
Oldcastle
County Meath
Ireland

www.gallerypress.com

ISBN 978 1 85235 499 2 *paperback*
       978 1 85235 500 5 *clothbound*

A CIP catalogue record for this book
is available from the British Library.

Contents

for Helen, Inor and Dallan
and in memory of
Peter Galligan,
musician and friend

1 *The Leavings*

Since I began to
look up

at your psalm
all of the instruments

have turned into birds. I cannot watch a man in song
    without wanting to draw his hand flung open.
With a pencil in the dark I mark the long neck of the cello
    that flies ahead like a swan.
The bass joins the banjo — they swing low over Carney —
    as the page turner

stands guard, ready to lean down and flick over when the
    pianist nods
at the waves. A skein rises offstage, and always out there to
    the left
is the straggler, the lone straggler, a violinist flying in from
    the side, eyes darting from the script,

to the quartet,
then back to the page to fill in the grave

as he leans to the left with one shoe jumping
on the ear of a spade.

What to do with the umbrella?
Lay it in the aisle?

Stand it on the knee-rest?
Lay it out on the seat?

Instead the soldier rests his forehead on it in prayer, as the
	footsteps of communicants
go to and fro to the tap of the hymn, keeping time in shoes,
heels, coughs, steps, the slow shuffle

and poignant sounds of little knocks from afar.
A woman's firm heel. Quilts, coats; the echoes gather up
in a tremolo as the priest approaches the silent box on wheels,

tripping on a foot-rest as he goes.
Then the soldier in front salutes,

lifts his chin off the head of the umbrella
and, with a whisper, kneels.

A little finger
and one thumb

pick at the bass, and send
a line that drums

from the tip of the bow across to the lamp in the corner.
Another quick thread goes up and down the thrashing hair
of the singer as she faces into the screech,

mouth open, dress to the side. Away to the left, in the dark
    on the cliff, sits
the other singer whose turn has yet to come. And as she
    listens to the hum
of baroque her unflinching eyes are constantly fixed above
    our heads

on the lighthouse
out the rock of John,

turning off,
turning on.

In April when the first lobster
boat appears in the bay

laying pigs'
trotters in pots

offstage the orchestra of memory is tuning up in front of
    the scarecrow
for their final appearance. They edge closer in their frocks,
    and sweep and glide and land
in a rehearsal for leaving. We sit in our cars, or out the rocks,

in the dumb hall, ready for a signal that is never given. Fifty-
    seven swans
cross with a slow beating flag. The first swallow is on the
    horizon. Down in a hollow
the gaggle of geese gathers before the conductor who holds
    his stalk up, ready to begin.

There isn't a sound. Like nuns in shawls
the geese walk the mission

with white beads running
through their wings.

If you're
on the headland

and stop
to look

up, it's as if you were turning down the leaf
of a book, so you might know where you stopped
reading that evening the geese shot out into the dark.

The book remains unopened for months, a whole summer.
The story of what happened is left unfinished, till one day
you stand out there on the rocky V of the alt, the quilt is
    shook,

you look up, in the library of coincidence
and, by chance, find the leaf

turned down
at the sound of the mark.

They knit joy
to terror

north of the torn seam.
The needle travels

through the evening sky as they come in beautiful stitches
along a thread, and another thread. The fire is lit.
Memory is at the gate and waves time through.

We gather in the ticking reeds, the fork of wind, the leap of
    the white mare
and stand by the battered gable trying to get our breath
for the journey that's left,

all of us
trying

to enter
the receding waters anew.

This was his jawbone.
This was his bed.

Here are his ashes,
hard now as lead.

The hills sit on an horizon made of clouds. The sea was a fire
that her hand lit. His seeds are pebbles. The head of the
   black bush rises into the blue.
Her offspring slope up against the sky and walk like camels

into the inlet. His white skull is a torch under the heap of
   shale.
The goose looks down on her shadow, the air is cold,
the dog rises off his rock, the moon tide rushes, we down
   tools

and go indoors
to light fires

from the leavings of a story
that cannot be told.

Out of the nest
they're dropped,

from the side
of a frozen cliff

into the surge. A few days after the longest day in the year
it happens. If they make it past the stones into the water
the story of two homes is told in rings. Then begins the long
   purge

of who will last the journey from Greenland to the other site
   of the Sound.
They fly in the same script as the parent, learning to share
   the lead
and make the V, like the alt, or the boat, and face into a wind
   that howls.

The mother is a hieroglyphic
in the grass. A sister is a honk in the void

as the orchestra of memory
takes to the air.

That
is history

going over
on the wing.

Listen to the echo of the gaggle flying straight into
    forgetfulness!
The same journey is made, again and again, by a wild goose,
    tamed by centuries
of wind, which sets the hands on the clock, year after year, to
    map out remembrance and bring

the unsure knowledge
to the door of the ruin on another island.
And, then, enters the new beginning. The long silence.

The last singing;
the splash of incense

that signals absence;
and over there the soft carpet of reeds that leads, at last, to
    sleep.

The chiefs
came back

in October
to turn over

the clay for spring, to set the bent and weed the earth.
I walked the horse and worked till all my breath was spent.
The flying column went back to sea. I turned the soil.

Then I waited on the steps below the altar
for the next command. But next morning the chiefs took
    another route
and found their way, each day, out of sound, inland,

while I slept late
with the bell in my hand

and a small congregation of missioners
walked the cloister on the misty ocean.

2 *The Sound of Time Flying*

A tied stone
is an angry dog.

A moored yacht
travels far

in a fog. The last tune of the night was 'The Geese in the Bog'.
While they're away I work on the beach, according to advice
I got from a man whose name I can't remember.

The clouds build. A lone musician sets up his keyboard
on driftwood. The heron, like a single note, stands for hours
at the edge of the mirror. The sea is not now in a rage.

The drowned man
has his hands folded over his chest.

I lean over to throw
stones in a cage.

The sands
are running out.

Time drums
into your lungs.

Death is a memory of something that happened
when you were young. You spit out the grains at first light
and wash the body down. Wake, and eat, and step out to dig
    into the deep.

Up on the ski slopes this Christmas they are playing
golf. Each spring they ship back the sands
that were stripped off the Spanish strand in winter. I was
    asleep

watching the geese
weed the sky

as he breathed
his last.

In the cathedral in Cavan
a cough at the front

is answered
by a cough at the back,

there's mental singing throughout,
but when the organist stops at the end
the silence reels round the walls

and slams above our heads
like a ricochet, through all of the Twelve Stations,
until the final accommodation. They lift him, they raise him,

they gather him up, and stand uncertain
under the coffin, reaching out

to each other for support, before walking unsteadily
into a photograph he might have taken.

The door of the church in Maugherow
began flapping open

to let the coffin out.
The latecomers in the porch

study the tiles; they'd done this before; we nod
and stand aside; the choir inside sing on alone; I ran my
　　hand down
a frond of palm as the body was carried out into the
　　downfall.

At the gate we shook hands with the living. Then a delay.
Someone had blocked the road with cars after a wedding
　　party
the night before, so the empty hearse had to go

the long way
round

to get
to the end.

Toward Easkey
the mountains and shadows

are coming and going
from the doldrums

to the drumlins. The slope comes towards us, then away
into the mist. Outside the church he is balanced on six men's
    arms.
A sheet of cold rain from the coming storm

greets the mourners
who walk behind the shouldered coffin the half-a-mile
to the open grave. The priest begins a rosary as the spades

of neighbours begin
the filling in.

The work is done
by the third Mystery.

Some don't like
the sound of clay

on a coffin.
They'd rather it was done

after they'd gone back to Dublin. The first men start, the
    others
wait by the earth mound and count the clouts of clay
till their turn comes round. The souls shovelling speed into
    a blur

as they try to beat the approaching storm. The undertaker
    opens a black umbrella
at the Resurrection, and now each toss of clay is suddenly
    silent.
The earth on the spade grows wonderfully light as the clay
    pans out.

Then, at the final sign of the cross, the cemetery empties
as the priest, like the hand of a clock,

comes to rest,
at last, on nought.

3 The Beaten Sound

If I was to hear
a recording

of that hallowed sound
it would not bring back

the song I knew. You have to be there
in the actual place
listening to what can never be heard till the next time

the gaggles descend and, with a swoop, thrash out the old air
that leaves a sudden echo in the windswept silence;
and sends us on a fool's errand

to where the sought-for happens
once only

in the itinerary
of wings.

The past is the present tense
of the verb to be.

Proof is an old superstition.
There's nothing nicer

than to see a man in a long lounge chair knitting
while the bog cotton floats and clumps of trees drift
off the earth in a mist of reeds. Out of what burnt log

did come the burnt nail? The bird is a poor excuse
for becoming a recluse in some place like heaven.
I never felt such sadness watching a dog's tail. Time is flying.

The future is what
happened only the once.

It will begin again
just after the ending.

The rainbow bows
down to pray

above the whip
of the ocean;

the lips of the sea break loud on the rocks
while out beyond in the bay
another language is starting

as the geese rise after another sleepless night
and go their rounds like an old civilization
in a black frightened cry naming the lost ones

who did not make it
back to the island

where time stands
drying its wings.

I would love
to have the garden dug

and the shadow
chased away by prayer

and to know that each work will be ended
one day, but the new beginnings have begun
to stretch further than I can reach;

and here they are — not ambitions
or works of wonder, not even chores,
but plain dear labour I took on

to shore up the beach
against the storms; but the wall I built

to keep the sea out is keeping me in
amongst the pounding diction.

The stars
while away the hours

to the roars
of the waves coming in from another shore;

and the stone is a clock that keeps time from where it was
    driven
in a rushy place abounding in echoes — listen!
In the dark the argument gathers and seems to bring to an
    end what pulls us apart

by going somewhere out there to the start; the great-winged
    nightfall
of home grows buoyant and runs for miles along a furrow
dug into dense fields of foam

as the white stone
arrives from the north

on the day
the hour was added on.

Far from home
the freed fossils

of coral
tumbled

in the rising tides, then later travelled with the ice
up the mountains and on through the valleys
till they reached the heights

where they sat forgotten in old forts
to look back through the gap
at the distant equator

where their ancient parents
are laid out

in spiralling tropics
around the Serpent's Rock.

The first rock I had
in my hand today

had a hem of a dress
turned to the side;

it was split down the centre with the chalk line
of a crack in the sea. In my palm the second stone
rested like a calm ocean; next I lifted the remains of a parade

in a Brazilian street that the north-east wind had sharpened
    into a blade
to cut wheat. There was great give to the west the day
the forces hung a chiselled apron round the tall coral frond

of the fern I found
scored by winds

long gone silent at the storm
within the beaten sound.

The round stone
has been through it all

and sits, higher than all the rest,
above the sands

crowding round the walking sticks of the bent grass.
They have shaken off enemies on all sides
and lie content till the next tide.

Back on the beach sit the beautiful estranged —
the broken-backed, the misshapen,
the maimed. They make altars from the past. Baskets of elves

sit in their laps. Amethyst looks
into the eye of quartz

as wealth is measured out
aloud, again, in salt.

The cold snap
on the stairs

to the Chinese pagoda
is lit by a red bead

of Ecuadorean sunlight. A fog has settled on the temporal
    lobe
off Cloonagh. A warp in time stands to attention in a garden
of small lime rushes and loose wrack. Lookouts have fallen

asleep at the entrance to the cave. Inside, the shapes
wait for the fire to take. Here is an unattended bed. There an
    orphan.
This is a squall. The quake sits alone in a puddle. Spent.

From Duark comes the smell of burning kelp.
Up goes the whoosh

over the buckled wall
in the Night Field.

This is the calm
before the storm,

the arguments that started
before you were born.

This is the stone scalp torn from the head
of an alt in St John's. We speak in languages that carry
messages from the dead and hand on

our own into the silences that will never be read,
but are known to you as you bend your head low
and make the promises that time has kept.

Someone else said
it will have to stop. Someone else nodded,

then heard himself say
I'm not ready to go yet.

4 *The Thrashing Shadows*

I am carted out of sleep
searching for

a room, under these rooms,
at the back of those others

with their windows. Not the long room that sits over
    everything,
nor the small one put there by chance:
but the long room where souls gather to talk,

to take a breath before heading
back the way we came. Behind me the stones
are finding their place, and are sitting on their own weight
    at last.

The job is done,
but something is missing from the curve

that leads back upward
toward that first unspoken word.

I never speak your name
in your absence.

Once gone your sound is replaced immediately
by some other.

The word that flies in, like the minute hand, is never heard
until the bird is in the air over your head
bringing news of a lost dialect

in from the vast wastes of memory, then
the sound of the making up begins all over again.
A chant is heard of something forgotten

as the echoes
that spell

the sound
go silent.

All summer long
they attach themselves

to the keel of thought
and make the long journeys

you make without your knowing they're there. They stop at
   home
in your illness, accompany you to the place you fear most.
Unseen underwater, they are stuck fast to what will soon land,

and be forgotten; they are in the back of the mind as you
   saunter
through a graveyard of candles in Poznan.
They remain unlit in the dark of the house.

And sometimes, at night
in bed, the pillow below my head

seems a thousand goose
miles away.

You are the spit on the footpath
under the May bush,

the nightlight on the leaf
of the trembling poplar.

You hide in the white sandal of a child
that sits all summer long discarded on the pier.
You are the lost key

hanging from the gate. You surge out of the opera
on the radio as I take the corner. Then there's nothing —
and yet you nearly existed for a moment

when my pen was let
form again

the first letter
of that alphabet.

And who was with you back then?
I think of the seagull

with a broken wing standing in the same spot for days
with one low dark eye

fixed on the sky. I remember the swan
that landed from a great height onto the frozen ice
and careered across the very image of herself,

screaming. With a broken leg
she roosted in pain on the white waters while her mate ran
the beach over and back, with terrible swooping cries ...

The swan at last rose
and fell, and slipped, then rose again out of

the thrashing shadows
as the gull died.

The heron,
ancient and slow,

was taking off
to land

with the cormorant, and the hare, on a rock. On a spit of salt
there they stand. The minute hand. 'Tom Ward's Downfall'.
The second hand. The swallows nod before sleep.

The young starlings cluck on the barbed wire.
The whins are lit. On St John's Eve the fires take. The
    evenings are long
and, just before dark, places are set at the Table of Listening

as the search starts
among the constellations

for the song
of the missing.

I imagine
the 3,000

wake as one
thinking it has started,

only to find
it's the short trip inland
that's ahead of them.

Another day. Not Greenland. The stars are unpicking
    themselves
as the geese wheel in
across the thundering sea

into a sudden script
that's read

by many
an upturned head.

Sometimes
they look

like that first ungainly structure
of DNA;

and sometimes they look
like the dying man's view of himself
as the soul lifts up out of the body:

this is myself lifted up above me,
the brain's flower aloft,
and again there is a point

to everything. With a raucous
call the birds head on

and hit the alt
with a vigorous, unyielding chant.

I'm out of here,
I said, and I went in,

and I went right up
into the light,

leaving that body below
that they were arguing over.
Let them have me.

I could think about anything up there.
Things were shown to me.
It all made sense again.

Then sadly I was returned into my body.
And it was painful.

I went back in
with my head on fire.

The everyday goes on.
I am who I am,

opening a can
to paint a toilet wall,

afraid of my folly first thing in the morning
and glad to welcome the postman
and put the sausages on.

No reflections in the cup of tea.
The cells go on copying themselves
without my knowing. Lorries take to the roads, the first call
    comes over the phone,

but before long
it starts.

As I pass a tree, or stone,
I'm no one.

5 *The Voyage*

The worst is the flat
calm sea

with the swell
gathering

away out there among the openings.
Down on the beach the gabions in the middle of the night
give a faraway groan as they sweep through the empty
    stations.

The trains in the dreams are forgotten in the sunlight next
    morning,
then across the peace comes the long huge white lift that
    arrives
without warning. Without wind. A storm in another land
    has been sent ahead

across the calms.
At the back door is the tornado in Florida

and further out are children, floating,
on a raft of psalms.

I thought I had got
through nice and handy,

the liver OK,
the kidney OK,

even the brain showed little signs of wear.
I knew the spine was weak at the top,
but I was told you can live with that.

Then up came the lungs in the X-ray,
two half moons in fog, blurred, badly drawn; the one thing
    I'd forgotten
that I'd always expected:

that some day
I might breathe

till the last, quickly,
like my father.

Poor comes the signal
as the winds grow strong

and tiredness climbs down
the veins of the temple

into the nest of the body where no fight is left.
After gauging the distance out from land
the Captain stripped down to his vest and went

below deck to bed, after setting the prow
direct into the eye of the storm. He lifted the vodka to his
    lips;
the Filipino sailors climbed in fear into the one bunk.

And while they slept
the unmanned wheel

held to its course, with the boat facing forward,
as it headed back to the place they'd set out from.

For two
long years, girl,

you travelled
in that boat.

Each morning brought another storm.
Each morning you expected to find yourself
thrust back on land

shipwrecked and lifeless.
And one night as you slept on that lone voyage in the dim
    ward
a Filipino nurse was brushing your hair

with such tenderness
and care

as she combed back in the curls
you'd combed away.

I have been
to that place I set

my mind upon,
and would climb it again

in the morning, knowing those footprints ahead of me
mark the trail I made coming down
from the heights. My absence

marks the spot where I stopped to take a breath.
This mound of earth is where I took in the sights.
These are your footprints. You never once complained

or sought anyone
to blame

as we all stood
too near the flame.

Storms are promised
that never come,

and some not promised
that do.

They come out of the blue,
out of the blue
because they are true,

because they are true.
Oh, they are true
to their word,

the storms not promised,
and they wreck you.

They wreck you,
they do.

A thousand years
of waiting

in the Goose Field.
Out the rocks

a thousand rogue waves: the one that caught
the lighthouse keeper
fishing mackerel,

that drowned the town man and his child
below the alt. The rogue wave
is waiting far out at sea

for all of us. Watch out!
It comes on your blind side,

just as you're
casting.

Overhead
an arrowhead of stars

follows after
an arrowhead of geese,

both shot from the one bow
that is no more.
The stars that appear forever

hover there directing the flight
of the geese to the island.
Here is the tune. This is the path, this is the way, they say,

and keep the faith
as you cross

the Jealous Wall, built from the ruins
of the Invisible Room.

In the cold rain
and the wind blowing inland

the geese lines
break down into blots.

They are no longer going to map out
the beginning of life;
to get home is uppermost.

They stand in the air in the wind.
How many wingbeats is it back to the island?
They fly in between one burst and the next.

They cry
like uncoiled springs.

The flap of their wings
tell the code is lost.

At four o'clock
they're scattering to the side

above the cliff
as they veer

back inland. One boat of birds
nearly twenty long man the oars
and are borne roughly

into the next windstorm, till they break apart,
to shelter in the Goose Field.
They are frantic and mad. The land is electric and, stepping
    out

of an unfinished life,
I can feel it under my feet —

that trolling rush
above my head.

There are people to count
the birds.

And people to count
the stars.

The stars increase
as the telescope peers further out
into the long years of space.

As the universe extends the birds grow less
as the people who watch them grow in numbers. The bird-
    watchers
hear before they see. They map the sound, search the reeds

until the binoculars
pin down the last of a kind

which is the first of a species
starting another existence.

If God did not exist
there would be no unbelievers.

If God did exist
there would be no believers.

We have not been here before in this place
and yet we have, in this life,
and nestled down

and made a home in someone else's home
who moved into the house we had left, as we all travelled
    back
to meet, for the first time again,

what will be taken
from us

to haunt the senses
in the years ahead.

6 *The Wild Goose Chase*

Open the front door
the back slams shut.

The past is at me.
It sits on my shoulder. The back is at me.

It sits on the shoulder of the Uncle who is haunting the
    future for signs.
The Aunt is content to become the pet
after living in the wild so long.

The Cousin, that wild creature, whom we have yet to meet,
is being tamed at the altar
before being released into the unknown.

Lift a wet stone today in the bitter cold and it's light to the
    touch.
Lift it in the warm morning and it will have grown heavy
    and blunt.

Open the front door
the back slams shut.

This chair I sit on,
this screen

I face,
those things I've done

will all have to be faced into again.
Where I will be tomorrow is already over.
The sorrow that turns to joy

leads us on a journey, shoulder to shoulder,
out to the island chapel
where the congregations of geese in thousands teach the
    shadows

that our first lie
to ourselves

was that the way ahead
had not already happened.

Everyone has
a wild goose

in the head
that they heard

once on the quiet border between Spain and France
or a balcony with Mongolian chanters in Perth,
the sweep to aft on a half-deck

at Aughris, or in a melodeon out the pier at Sopot,
a main street in Prague by an empty tomb.
In some back room

long forgotten
a goose

is about to spread
its wings.

The absence
grows from one

day to the next.
You are not there

at first light to answer the call.
Or water has battened down
the bird, while your feet enter the world

of the absurd. All is dark. The text is in shreds
as a few waves beat to the shore of the slanted beach.
The wind is shaking the car.

The here,
and the now,

holding on to each other,
have travelled far.

The beginning
and the end

are old friends.
They don't take

passengers beyond a certain point.
There is a rule — the time you live, in the long run,
is the best. Forget the rest, the debt is paid. Anything else

is sentiment. We invent anew an old arrogance.
So the man in the 7th century took the man in the 3rd for
    a fool.
The woman in the 12th had little time for the handmaid in
    the back

row at school. The 21st
sees the rest as cursed.

And the scientist in the 30th
will see us as the worst.

Our ego
can't wait,

even as the present,
with a shrug,

drops us off some windy Wednesday at the cemetery gate.
The new day sits into the driving seat, adjusts the mirror,
and looking back goes forward, in a vehicle that does not yet
    exist.

We will put an end to that poverty of mind
that you missed, as the universe lay all around you
unfound, say the mathematician and the monk

as they bid
for the pattern

that began
at the start.

And so
I am aware

that this sadness
may not be here tomorrow;

that the words I speak I owe to some other;
that the questions they asked
will always form again in my mind

when I look up and see the geese fly over my head
as they've flown over the centuries, to bring the prayer to rest,
and carry the stop to the end of sentence,

the verb high
over the rock

and the noun
down, quietly, into the nest.

Even if
one morning

the geese are there
near the pond

next minute they've gone into the beyond.
Nor can the black-and-white picture keep those marvellous
    feet
tucked up against the smooth and ruffled

coat. The light from the lighthouse
says we are here, but the clock has stopped.
The song has stopped in the throat. Nothing is waiting

at the end
of the race

that started
the wild goose chase.

It's a fool's
errand

we began
at the end

of that first mission — to get up and do what we ought;
on the journey out going over and over again
what was needed; re-checking the future that we brought —

and then, going on fast with what we forgot till,
ahead, we meet what has already happened,
turn back at last to face into

the writing in the sky,
the galaxy of light years,

and whatever else can fit
into the past.

It's hard
to step out of the echo

of all that's happened
and all that will,

the winter nights that sent you to the gable
to listen beyond the spit of salt to hear
the troubled chant of all who go

the Sky Road, built by a wave that rowed from a place
where communication broke down, that sent
this prayer of birds to brave the weather

and reach
our ears

with the passing sound
of forever.

For some
it's the sea,

the boat,
the mountain top,

the moment when the crying stopped,
the room at the top of the city stair where youth was spent,
the amen at the end of the prayer, the despair,

a violin, a dog, a roof, the empty boat on
the Amazon, a pocket in an overcoat, the students' ball,
what song it was wrote those notes into the throat

that started
the mime

of silence
down in Salvation Hall.

I found the Crucifixion
on a small stone.

The cloths of the man
on the cross were blowing

in exact lines, as were the cloths of the crouched penitent
at his feet. I tossed the holy pebble aside to lift a rock into
    place (I'll get it later)
and then headed home, stopped, and went back to begin the
    search. I handled straw,

veins, and spine. I found a skull with a key for an ear in the
    manuscript of gravel.
I went over and back, knowing in my heart it was lost, the
    ink line of flint
that the mason of movement had drawn on a seed

with a nib dipped in quiet rage.
It was meant for my mantelpiece.

That night a bomb in Baghdad
cleared the old lettering off another page.

The scattered runes
on the break,

and longer aloft
the scattered remains

of webbed heraldry. The shield, the fur. Horsetail, vexillium.
Not a stir from all the white-sheeted flags lost in the field
after another surrender. Tapping his foot like a musician

Achates aches on the shore at his parting from Aeneas.
The war is lost; there are none to save. Justice leaves.
With one roar of a wave the beach is swept clean.

Peace is declared till the next high tide.
Out on the wires the starlings sit,

ready to build
their nests in the eaves.

Night has fallen
but the gaggle did not sing,

the sky ended in silence.
With no one to call me in

I worked on feeding the seeds into a furrow I could not see.
From the first sprouting potato to the fall of the sycamore
    leaf
on the Road to the Crows the turn in the sky will happen on
    another shore.

Each evening the silence grows longer. The scattering has
    stopped.
Mid-April. We live in a chapel of salt. I dig in the last and
    find
myself alone in the garden. There was no foreman in the sky

to call quit. No sudden
enchantment to ease

my conscience. It was
their song I was working for.

7 *The Late November List*

If I had never looked up into the skies
or heard your sad triumphant cries,

oh gosling, goose, barnacle!
I still think you go back

into the past, with your wing-beating,
fierce left-handed sound,
to a pub in Leitrim

at closing time
where the men are
calling out their goodbyes

to ghosts
who believe in humans

because
they die.

To really sleep,
which I can't,

you have to settle
on a sober island

with your flying finished;
put down your wings,
and scratch a bit there.

Don't move towards her.
Or think of air. The conductor has
put the baton down. If you are a she or a he

don't be.
Of course you are not a bird.

The chattering fret is out beyond
on the White Martyrdom.

The thing to do
is to forget

that there is no rest
once you've set out.

The weather shoves you on.
You are not one but many
at the same place listening

for the first time again
to hear that late November
list in the dark,

that ocean-loud disturbance
out the back

as the wandering line of scholars
flies past.

The howl in the bowel
is on

as I hear suddenly
the geese going in.

Just a small trek to the left
of memory
on an unlit road

over the whins.
Put down the pen.
Sleep.

They are shouting —
'I am alive,

despite
everything!'

At half-past four
they come spilling

in twos and fours,
a swinging fifth

in wild symmetry to make the shape of a fish,
then for one astounding moment
the lines sketch a huge bird with long thin winding wings

and suddenly the bird becomes
a jester, with cap and nose
and flying cloak,

as they break
over the sea

taking the vowel sounds
with them.

While the birds bed down
the stars gently

beat their wings
searching the earth below

for a place
to land sometime
after this long

night flight
over everything
is finished.

The movement of the stars
is infinitesimal

as they climb the stairs
to the opening.

From gaggle to skein
every evening

and next morning
back again

shouting directions to the next in line.
Even on the earth they make a pattern
of leaving, that near sunset

is a ribbon of birds
tied to the dark dot of a leader
taking the thread out into the unseen.

Two souls sit in a boat.
They thrash the air,

then, with one last stroke,
the whoosh spreads over the gingley of auger and augite.

8 The Arrowhead

At evening the geese
make way for the stars

and at morning
the stars

turn into a flock of souls
that face back
into the mainland

to scatter
the geese grass on borrowed land
till again they weed the heavens

and, come dark,
they turn

with one last whoop
into stars.

Shot from the one bow
that is no more

the birds
grow frantic

as their time comes
to leave the island
behind them for the Atlantic.

Forays are made,
they lose their way, argue.
Leaders falter beyond the cliff

as the stars
grow more rigid

in the direction
they have to go.

For weeks in April
the scolding goes on

and on till one morning
at daybreak

the birds do not appear.
The sky is suddenly quiet.
They're gone.

I am that night
watching the island on the horizon
when suddenly

a few bright stragglers
back on the shaft

honk a great wild
encouragement.

Each side of the leader
flares are lit.

The arrowhead
that's been buried

beneath a bank of clouds
shoots out into the night
and points

towards the Path of the Birds.
All night they wait to take off
along the Sea Road

with one long silent screech
and no nest or rest

in the deep
waste.

Silence begins
as nights shorten.

In the fields
the clock has stopped

on the hour. Oystercatcher,
gull, snipe, curlew
are at it.

So are the sparrow and the wren.
But evening and morning
have lost

the birds
that announce

the dark
in one long meandering line.

Then comes October
when memory

is released.
The white-headed monks

have ridden from the North over driftwood and limpet
without stopping,
back to Innishmurray island,

come trumpeting singly
in from the sea
and, with fearful shrieks,

land,
and stand, facing back

the way
they came.

A psalm of geese
labours overland

cajoling each other
near half-one

on the day war started.
The din grew immense.
No need to look up.

All you had to do
was sit in the sound
and put it down

as best you could.
In from the sea came

a small airplane.
I waved.

Then comes the day
they pass overhead unnoticed —

a rich warm day.
You're thinking of other things,

to get something done
right to the end, see
something finished and, in a break

from lifting stone, sit looking inland
where life goes on.
Then, just before dark,

they break overhead in thousands
with a marvellous

pouring of song
into the beyond.

The beyond can belong
to the past:

this I see
as now is nearly over.

But later in my bed
a swan goes over the house
I grew up in.

A silence comes down.
The dog nods at something
in her sleep. The sea wind

is gathering
at the gable.

When the engine stops
that's when you wake.

You learn to sleep
to the beat of the engine

and wake when
it stalls

on the way to the shot. It's the silence gets you
after the worst has passed the walls. When the high banking
    sea
ceases and the sound is gone

to another shore you wake and sweep the debris off the road,
shovel away the gravel,
or sit on the edge of the bed

wondering what was it
that happened

all those moments
before the pistons stopped.

The geese say
when to rest,

to leave that other stone
till morning,

and when to rise, and when you've slept in late.
Five minutes before dark,
five minutes after light,

they begin the prayer.
When you miss the morning song
you know you've done wrong. Then they take away your
    conscience

and it's strange
how at a given moment

you look up
and listen with dreadful longing.

9 *The Ebbing Song*

For six months
there'll be no long

wandering wave coming in over the sea
to announce

start of day.
Sometime soon the day will end
without the barnacles going out with the tide.

Even before they go
they've gone. Somewhere in March
it starts.

One faraway
blow of a hammer

and the Goose Field
rises yelling into the air.

It's not a lonesome sound
but a panic,

a calling out to the others
to see if they're there;

it's not the lung-full thrust of the prong of arrival
in late October;
not the slow togetherness

of the shape they take
on the empty land
on the days before Christmas:

this is different, this is a broken family,
the young go the wrong way,

then, at daybreak, rise up and follow their elders again filled
    with dread
at the returning sound of the journey ahead.

By evening they are an army
come back

after losing the battle,
lone soldiers

shouting out their distress
as they search for their company,
scattered in a gale.

A group of ten
charges before dark
back behind the enemy lines

to the island;
then, in little lots, come the others

without once
looking behind.

A deserted island
is the right place

for such birds
to spend their nights:

they waited years for the humans
to pack up and go. Out on Innishmurray
they nestle under St Molaise's stiff skirt, move the letters

of the old alphabet on foot towards the monk's beehive hut.
The church of the Men and the church of the Women
are filled with evening song.

The quarrel before sleep
is heard by few.

There's silence
around the Cursing Stones.

The little we have
needs praising.

Some have to starve
themselves to stay alive.

A woman with Alzheimer's
is flirting madly in Surgical 2.
She was always into the men,

her niece explains. A vodka and tonic
first thing in the morning
is nice, ah very nice. But there's no hope in

sitting in the house waiting on the pub to open,
so building a drystone wall in Lent is good.

And please don't talk till three on Good Friday.
Work finetunes the instrument.

The notion of going
has started.

You can see it in them.
Time is on the move.

You see,
with a secret desire
to remember.

Maybe you will, maybe you won't.
A lot goes out the back door.
Some things are tidied away for good

without your knowing.
I like to look up

and see them
after they've gone.

The hare
burnt by the sun

is up the shore.
He has a path beaten

through the bent to perch again on the rock with the heron.
The ass is dead. The ass is buried and his bray has gone up
into the far reaches of memory to echo down the throat of
    his grieving friend.

One night on Lough Oughter the trees exploded beyond
    the castle.
There was chaos about the Pleasure House as the geese rose.
Last night the lights on the arcade of leaves were again
    switched on.

Next morning out on the wires the starlings sit
facing us again, with a deep chortling hum,

as they build, with short darts,
another wonderment. One goes, one comes.

At times
a fleet of ducks

flies by
in your column.

I see someone going down a street who has another's footsteps,
his shoulders, his chin. I see my brother's shape going slow,
    with a shopping bag,
up a road he never stood on. In San Francisco

I meet a lot of old friends that have never been there —
his corr, her glance aside at my passing.
An old soul leans down to tie a shoe. The harder it gets to
    recall

a face from the past
the more people I meet that I knew

who now live on
in the face of a stranger.

Today
they've grown tidy,

the wave of the line is perfect,
the cries

are not fearful, they know
where they are going:
the weather is right.

What more could you ask for?
And when they hit the sea
the chorus stops.

We do not hear them.
They take their song with them.

This is the one certainty —
that ebbing song.

Acknowledgements

Acknowledgements are due to the editors of *Cathach, Forty, The Irish Times* and *The Moth* in which some of these poems were published first.

I would like to thank Fintan Vallely for all his musical help over the years and Martin Enright for sharing his visual and historical records of the barnacles.